Affiliate Marketing Blueprint

Jim Stephens

Published by RWG Publishing, 2021.

While every precaution has been taken in the preparation of this book, the publisher assumes no responsibility for errors or omissions, or for damages resulting from the use of the information contained herein.

AFFILIATE MARKETING BLUEPRINT

First edition. October 29, 2021.

Copyright © 2021 Jim Stephens.

Written by Jim Stephens.

Also by Jim Stephens

Kindle Publishing Made Easy: Autopilot Cash With Amazon Kindle!
Million-Dollar Secrets of the Amazon Associates: How They Make Money From the Biggest Online Shopping Mall
Self-Publishing Made Easy: The Easy Way to Self-publish Your Own Books!
Scam Busters: How to Avoid the Most Popular Scams of Today!
Affiliate Marketing and Blogging
The Quick and Easy Guide of Diamonds
Government Information
Hiking and Camping
Koi Pond
Law Information Guide
Motor Homes Research
Affiliate Marketing and Success Systems
Online Shopping
Outsourcing Ebooks and Software Jobs
Personal Loans
Private Jet Charters
Private Yacht Charters
Affiliate Marketing Blueprint

Table of Contents

Affiliate Marketing Introduced... 1
The 3 Things All Affiliate Marketers Need To Survive Online........... 7
Instructions to Become A Super Affiliate In Niche Markets............ 11
How can one turn into an effective affiliate in the specialty markets utilizing web facilitating?... 13
Such countless Affiliate Programs! Which One Do I Choose?...... 15
Which Affiliate Networks To Look Out For When Promoting.... 19
Why take part in an affiliate program?... 21
Simple Profits Using PPC In Your Affiliate Marketing Business.... 25
Utilizing Product Recommendations To Increase Your Bottom Line... 29
Utilizing Camtasia to Increase Your Affiliate Checks....................... 33
Top 3 Ways To Boost Your Affiliate Commissions Overnight........ 37
Instructions to Avoid The 3 Most Common Affiliate Mistakes..... 41

Affiliate Marketing Introduced

Being in the affiliate displaying business isn't that troublesome now with the Internet at your nonessential. It is significantly easier now diverged from the days when people need to use the telephones and various instruments of information just to get the latest reports on the way their program is coming.

So with development nearby, and tolerating that the affiliate is working from home, a day in their life would sound something like this...

Subsequent to arousing and in the wake of eating, the PC is proceeded to check out new upgrades in the association. Considering all that there might be new things to invigorate and estimations to keep track on.

The site design should be changed. The sponsor understands that an especially arranged site can grow initiates from visitors. It can in like manner help in the affiliate's change rates.

That done, the opportunity has arrived to introduce the affiliate program to files that summaries affiliate programs. These records are means to attract people in joining your affiliate program. A positive technique for propelling the affiliate program!

Time to discover the business you are getting from your affiliates sensibly and unequivocally. There are phone demands and ships off find. Check whether they are new clients taking a gander at the things. Observing down the contact information that might be a plausible source later on.

There are heaps of resources for sort out. Advancements, principles, button promotions and test ideas to give out considering the way that the publicist understands that this is one strategy for ensuring more arrangements. Best to stay perceptible and accessible too.

The affiliate sponsor remembered that there are requests to address from the visitors. This should be done quickly. Nothing can unwind a customer than an unanswered email.

To exhibit that the affiliate is working effectively and capably, solicitations would should be centered nearer around. Nobody should be ignored and customers are not by and large the most agreement, things being what they are. Quick answer that should appear to be capable yet agreeable also.

During the time spent doing all of the necessities, the sponsor is endorsed on to a visit room where the individual being referred to helps out various affiliates and those under that identical program. This is where they can discuss things on the most capable technique to best propel their things.

There are things to be learned and it is a steady association. Sharing tips and advices is a respectable technique for showing support. There may be others out there expecting to join and may be enamored by the discussion that is proceeding. There is no naughtiness in expecting what openings ahead.

The leaflets and E-zines were revived days earlier, so it is the best chance for the affiliate sponsor to check whether there are some new things happening keeping watch. This will be explained in the promoter's dispersion to be passed on to the old and new customers.

These comparable conveyances are moreover a huge instrument in keeping awake with the most recent with the as of late introduced things. The promoter has set up an arrangement and progression that customers may have to ponder. Also, they need to remain mindful of the cutoff season of these arrangements written in the conveyances.

It is that opportunity to show some appreciation to individuals who have helped the promoter in the progressions and arrangement increase. Not the slightest bit like referring to individuals, their regions and the collaboration they have done that made everything worked.

Clearly, this will be disseminated in the flyers. Among the more critical information that have been made as out of now.

The promoter really has the chance to work out ideas to individuals who need valid focal points for the things being progressed. There is similarly an optimal chance to post a couple of comments on the most capable strategy to be a powerful affiliate sponsor on a site where there are lots of wannabes.

Two objections done all the while. The promoter will propel the thing similarly as the program they are in. Who knows, someone may be inclined to join.

Time elapses rapidly. Missed lunch anyway is extremely happy with the tasks done. Bed time....

Okay, so this may not be totally done in a day. Anyway by then, this furnishes you with a considered how an affiliate sponsor, a serious one that is, spends the advancing day.

Is that accomplishment moving toward some place distant without a doubt?

The 3 Things All Affiliate Marketers Need To Survive Online

By and by each affiliate promoter is ceaselessly looking for the productive market that gives the best check. Every so often they think it is a charm condition that is expeditiously open for them. In light of everything, it is more jumbled than that. It is essentially adequate advancing practices that have been exhibited over significant length of troublesome work and dedication.

There are procedures that have worked before with online elevating and is continuing to work in the web based affiliate promoting universe of today. With these principle three exhibiting tips, you will really need to prepared to grow your arrangements and make due in the affiliate advancing on the web.

What are these three techniques?

1. Using fascinating site pages to propel each unique thing you are publicizing.

Make an effort not to lump each and every piece of it together to get a decent arrangement on web working with. It is ideal to have a site focusing in on each and every thing and that is it.

Constantly fuse thing reviews on the site so visitors will have a hidden understanding on how the thing can manage individuals who gets them. In like manner fuse recognitions from customers who have successfully endeavored the thing. Be sure that these customers are anxious to allow you to use their names and photos on the site of the specific thing you are advancing.

You can in like manner form articles including the livelihoods of the thing and recall them for the site as an additional a page. Make the pages engaging persuading and recall calls to address the information. Each component should attract the perusers to endeavor to examine more, even contact you. Component your excellent core interests. This will help your perusers with understanding what's new with the page and should find more.

2. Offer free reports to your perusers.

In case possible position them at the very top side of your page so it they fundamentally can't be missed. Endeavor to make autoresponder messages that will be shipped off individuals who input their own information into your sign up box. As demonstrated by research, an arrangement is closed commonly on the seventh contact with a chance.

Only two things may maybe happen with the site page alone: concluded arrangement or the chance leaving the page and never return again. By setting supportive information into their inboxes not really set in stone period, you will assist them with recalling the thing they thought they need later and will find that the arrangement is closed. Be sure that the substance is directed toward unequivocal inspirations to buy the thing. Do whatever it takes not to make it sound like an endeavor to sell something.

Focus in on huge centers like how your thing can make life and things more straightforward and really beguiling. Recollect persuading titles for the email. Whatever amount as could sensibly be anticipated, make an effort not to use "free" because there are at this point more prepared spam channels that dumps those kind of substance into the trash before even anyone scrutinizing them first. Convince individuals who sought after your free reports that they will be missing something significant if they don't benefit of your things and organizations.

3. Get the kind of traffic that is assigned to your thing.

Basically think, if the person who visited your site has no interest at all in what you are offering, they will be among individuals who forge ahead and stay away forever. Form articles for dispersion in e-zines and e-reports. This way you can discover appropriations that is focusing in on your target customers and what you have set up may grab their benefit.

Endeavor to create somewhere around 2 articles every week, with something like 300-600 words in length. By reliably creating and staying aware of these articles you can deliver as much as 100 assigned perusers to your site in a day.

Constantly review that primary 1 out of 100 people are presumably going to buy your thing or get your organizations. If you can make as much as 1,000 assigned hits for your site in a day, that infers you can made 10 arrangements subject to the typical estimation.

The methodologies given above doesn't really amazing very testing to do, all things being equal. It just requires a concise period and a movement expect your part.

Endeavor to use these tips for seemingly forever publicizing programs. You can end keeping a good sort of income and making due around here that not all that publicists can do.

Moreover, contemplate the enormous checks you will get!

Instructions to Become A Super Affiliate In Niche Markets

Over the previous years, web facilitating has become greater than it used to be. With more organizations getting into this business and tracking down the many advantages it can give them, the interest for web facilitating has never been higher. These appear to be the pattern of today.

38 million individuals have set up their absolute first sites online this year 2005 alone. It is assessed that by 2008, the Internet deals industry will top the dollar bank. Also, to figure, larger part of those locales will offer distinctive affiliate programs for individuals to pick and take an interest into.

This main method a certain something. It is simpler now to track down the right web have for your application. The chance of value web facilitating organizations isolating themselves from the remainder of the business is expected. In case this is done, the amateurish and inept ones will endure.

Backing will be the main thought for individuals while picking a web have. It will be clear that customary publicizing will turn out to be less and less compelling. A great many people would prefer to choose the web have dependent on things that they see and hear. Likewise dependent on the suggestions by the people who have attempted them and have ended up being an effective.

This is an extraordinary chance for web facilitating affiliates and affiliates the same. There would many web facilitating and projects to look over that the trouble in tracking down the right one for them isn't an issue any longer.

How can one turn into an effective affiliate in the specialty markets utilizing web facilitating?

Checking out this intelligently, every single person who needs a website needs a web working with association to have it for them. Now, there is in reality no driving working with industry so by far most pick has based from recommendations. When in doubt, they get it from the ones that have successfully benefited of a web working with organizations.

With the many hosts offering affiliate programs, there is the tendency to find the one which you think will end up being brutal for you. Contemplate the thing you will progress. Model them to the site and check whether they are considering the very same things as you are.

Right when you have been with one host for a significant length of time and have all the earmarks of being not to advance a lot in any case the aggregate of your endeavor, leave that one and quest for another. There is no use in endeavoring to stick to one when you would be before off in another. Things will simply have to improve starting there since you at this point have been in most extremely awful conditions.

Try this out. On the off chance that you are exceptionally lively and content with your web have, endeavor to check whether they are offering an affiliate program you can share on. Maybe than you paying them, why not make it the converse way around; them paying you. The cycle can be just comparably basic as putting somewhat "powered by" or "worked with by" associate at the lower part of your page and you are at this point in an affiliate business.

Why pick paying for your for your web working with when you don't have to? Endeavor to get repaid by telling people you like your web have.

Constantly review that while picking a web have, pick the one that is known for its great customer care. There are moreover many working with affiliate programs. Remaining affiliate program is similarly being worked with. This is the program wherein you get remunerated a rate every month for a client that you insinuate. This can allow you to have a reliable kind of income. With consistent quality, you can even be exceptionally productive in this field.

There are a huge load of strength features out there just believing that the right affiliate will invade to them and make that dollars dream work out. Knowing which one to get into is being sure enough of your potential outcomes and the incredible results you will get.

Web working with is just one affiliate market you could test and make some extraordinary and industrious compensation. Just remember that to be powerful on your endeavor moreover suggests that time, effort and resistance is required.

Nobody has made the ideal affiliate market yet. Regardless, certain people do acknowledge how to turn out to be stunningly effective in this kind of market. It is essentially knowing your kind of market and making the pay there.

Such countless Affiliate Programs! Which One Do I Choose?

Posture requests first before you join an affiliate program. Do a little research about the choices of program that you hope to join into. Track down a couple of arrangements since they will be the picking point of what you will achieve later on.

Will it cost you anything to join? Most affiliate programs being offered today are absolutely to no end. So why settle for those that charge you a couple of dollars before joining.

When do they give the commission checks? Each program is novel. Some issue their truly investigates the twofold per month, each quarter, etc Select the one that is fit to your portion time choice. Many affiliate programs are setting a base procured commission total that an affiliate should meet or outperform all together for their checks to be given.

What is the hit per bargain extent? This is the ordinary number of hits to a norm or text interface it takes to make an arrangement reliant upon all affiliate bits of knowledge. This factor is basic because this will tell you how much traffic you ought to make before you can secure a commission from the arrangement.

How are references from an affiliate's site followed and for how long do they remain in the structure? You ought to be sure on the program enough to follow those people you insinuate from your site. This is the fundamental way that you can credit for an arrangement. The time span that those people stay in the system is furthermore critical. This is because a couple of visitors don't tolerating from the get go yet may have to return later to make the purchase. Know whether you will regardless get credit for the arrangement on the off chance that it is done a couple of months from a particular day.

What are such affiliate subtleties available? Your choice of affiliate program should be prepared for offering positive subtleties. They should be open online at whatever point you decide to check out them. Ceaselessly checking your singular subtleties is crucial for know the quantity of impressions, hits and arrangements are presently made from your site. Impressions are the events the flag or text interface was seen by a visitor of your site. A hit is the one tapping on the banner or text joins.

Does the affiliate program also pay for the hits and impressions other than the commissions on bargains? It is huge that impressions and hits are furthermore paid, as this will add to the pay you get from the business commission. This is especially huge if the program you are in offers low arrangements to have the choice to hit extent.

Who is the web based retailer? Find whom you are working with to know whether it is really a solid association. Know the things they are selling and the typical total they are achieving. The more you contemplate the retailer offering you the affiliate program, the more straightforward it will be for you to know whether that program is genuinely for yourself just as your site.

Is the affiliate a one level or two level program? A singular level program pays you only for the business you, by the day's end, have delivered. A two level program pays you for the business, notwithstanding it moreover pays you a commission on the on the arrangements made by any affiliate you support in your program. Some two-level undertakings are regardless, paying little costs on each new affiliate you support. More like an enlistment charge.

All in all, what is the proportion of commission paid? 20% - 80% (and a couple of cases, 100%!) is the commission paid by most ventures. .01% - .05% is the total paid for each hit. In case you find a program that also pays for impressions, the total paid isn't much in any capacity. As you can see from the figures, you will by and by understand why the typical arrangements aggregate and hit to bargain extent is huge.

These are just a piece of the requests that required tending to first before you go into an affiliate program. You should be familiar with the various critical points that your picked program should have preceding combining them into your site. Endeavor to ask your affiliate program choices these requests. These can help you with picking the right program for you site from among the various available.

Which Affiliate Networks To Look Out For When Promoting

There are various frightening stories about affiliate undertakings and associations. People have heard them over and over, that some are even cautious about obliging one. The stories they may have heard are those related to unlawful undertakings or fake plans of action. Generally, this kind of market doesn't have veritable, admirable thing.

You would rather not be connected with these plans. It is clear you should be with a program that offers first class thing that you will quickly guarantee. The creating number of the people who have joined at this point and are succeeding tremendously is proof enough that there are strong and quality affiliate programs out there.

Why take part in an affiliate program?

It grants you to work low upkeep. It offers you the opportunity to build a liberal extra compensation. Additionally, it makes you an owner of an autonomous endeavor. Affiliate programs have at this point made heaps of moguls. They are the living announcement of how troublesome work; constant prospecting, energizing and setting others up pay off.

In the event that whenever you are deciding to oblige one, you ought to see that you are getting into something intended to what you can do. This will be an assertion that you can viably come out productive.

How might you pick a nice affiliate program to progress? The following are a couple of clues you may have to examine preceding picking one:

1. A program that you like and have interest in.

Likely the best technique for knowing whether that is the kind of program you wish to progress is on the off chance that you are enthusiastic about purchasing the thing yourself. In the event that that is the circumstance, chances are, there are various others who are furthermore propelled by comparative program and things.

2. Look for a program that is of first rate.

For instance, look for one that is connected with various experts in that particular industry. Thusly, you are ensured that of the standard of the program you will join into.

3. Join during the ones that offer veritable and appropriate things.

How might you know this? Do some basic investigation. If possible, discover a part of the people and customers to give you recognition on the legitimacy of the program.

4. The program that is considering a creating target market.

This will promise you that there will be more and constant solicitations for your references. Make demands. There are social affairs and discussions you can check out to get extraordinary and trustworthy reactions.

5. A program with a compensation plan that pays out an extra compensation and a payout of 40% or more would be an uncommon choice.

There are a couple of tasks offering this kind of pay. Search cautiously for one. Make an effort not to consume your involvement in programs that don't remunerate liberally for your undertakings.

6. Be aware of the base guidelines that you ought to fulfill or bargains center around that is too hard to even think about evening consider achieving.

Some affiliate programs powers pre-necessities before you get your installments. Essentially be sure that you are good for accomplishing their requirements.

7. Select one that has a great deal of instruments and resources that can help you with fostering the business in the most restricted possible time.

Not all affiliate programs have these cutoff points. Make use you choose one with heaps of obliging instruments you can use.

8. Check out if the program has an exhibited structure that can allow you to really investigate your associations and compensation.

Furthermore check if they have it open online for you to check at whatever point and wherever.

9. The program that is offering strong inspirations for people to re-energize their support each time.

The affiliate program that gives predictable help and climbs to its things will in general hold its people. These things can ensure the advancement of your associations.

10. Be aware of the things that people are agitated about in a program.

Like with the ones referred to above, you can do your checking at discussion conversations. If you know someone in that identical program, there is no harm inquisitive with respect to whether there are various disadvantages included.

Have a cautious and genuine data about the affiliate program and association you will progress on.

Knowing the kind of program you are winding up stirred up with will make you expect and hinder any future issues you may insight.

Simple Profits Using PPC In Your Affiliate Marketing Business

PPC or Pay-Per-Click in full is one of the four essential sorts of Search Engines. PPC is moreover one of the most monetarily keen techniques for assigned Internet advancing. According to Forbes magazine, PPC or Pay Per Click, records to 2 billion dollars each year and is depended upon to addition to around 8 billion dollars consistently 2008.

Permit us to examine how PPC Search Engines work.

These engines make postings and rate them subject to a bid aggregate the webpage owner will pay for each snap from that web searcher. Supporters bid against each other to get higher situating for a specific expression or articulation.

The most essential bidder for a particular watchword or articulation will then, have the site situated as number 1 in the PPC Search Engines followed continually and third most important bidder, up to the last number that have set a bid on a comparable expression or articulation. Your advancements then, will appear recognizably on the results pages reliant upon the dollar aggregate bid you will agree to pay per click.

How might you get cash by using PPC into your affiliate advancing business?

Most affiliate programs perhaps pay when an arrangement is made or a lead passed on after a visitor has clickthrough your site. Your pay will not for the most part be pretty much as old as will be dependent upon the site content and the traffic market.

The support for why you should combine PPC into your affiliate exhibiting program is that pay are easier to make than in another kind of affiliate program not using PPC. Thusly, you will make gain based from the clickthroughs that your visitor will make on the advertiser's site. As opposed to specific tasks, you are not paid per arrangement or movement.

PPC can be amazingly quick of your site. With PPC Search Engines combined into your affiliate program, you will really need to profit from the visitor's who are not enthused about your things or organizations. Comparative ones who leave your site and stays away forever.

You will not simply get commissions not simply from the people who are just glancing through the web and finding the things and organizations that they required at this point you will really need to build your website page's affirmation as a significant resource. The visitors who have found what they needed from you site are presumably going to return and review what you are offering even more eagerly. Then, they will eventually get back to examine the web for various things.

This kind of affiliate program is in like manner a straightforward way for you to deliver some more additional livelihoods. For example, when a visitor on your site does a request in the PPC Search Engine and snaps on the marketing specialist anticipated postings, the advertisers' record will then, be deducted because of that snap. With this, you will be reimbursed 30% to 80% of the advertisers' offered total.

PPC isn't only a wellspring of creating straightforward advantages; it can moreover help you with propelling your own site. An enormous piece of the activities grant the commissions had the chance to be gone through for advancing with them rapidly and with no base securing essential. This is one of the more fruitful methods of exchanging your unrefined visitors for assigned surfers who has more tendencies to purchase your things and organizations.

AFFILIATE MARKETING BLUEPRINT

What will happen if you when you arrange PPC into your affiliate program?

PPC regularly have arranged to-use affiliate gadgets that can be easily organized into your site. The most notable gadgets are search boxes, banners, text associations and some 404-botch pages. Most web crawlers utilize custom plans and can outfit you with a white-mark affiliate program. This engages you, using several lines of code, to consolidate remotely worked with co-checked web searcher into your webpage.

The key benefits? More money made just as some extra money as a bit of hindsight. Other than a lifetime commissions at whatever point you have implied some site administrator allies to the engine.

Think about it. Where might you have the option to get this heap of benefits while beforehand creating some compensation for your site? Knowing a piece of the more accommodating gadgets you can use for your affiliate program is certainly not a waste of time. They are genuinely a strategy for obtaining inside a getting.

Best look into how you can use PPC web lists into your affiliate program than miss a phenomenal opportunity to procure more advantages.

Utilizing Product Recommendations To Increase Your Bottom Line

In affiliate promoting, there are numerous manners by which you can build your income and keep up with the record that you have buckled down for as of now. The greater part of the methods and strategies can be adapted without any problem. No compelling reason to go anyplace and any further. They are accessible on the web, 24 hours per day and 7 days per week.

One of the more significant methods of expanding affiliate advertising main concern and deal is using item suggestions. Numerous advertisers realize that this is one of the best courses in advancing a specific item.

Assuming the clients or guests trust you enough, they will trust your suggestions. However, be extremely cautious in utilizing this methodology. In the event that you begin advancing everything by proposal, your believability will really wear ragged. This is seen particularly when proposals are apparently overstated and absent a lot of legitimacy.

Try not to be reluctant to make reference to things that you don't care for about a given item or administration. Maybe than lose any focuses for you, this will make your proposal more practical and will in general build your believability.

Besides, if your guests are truly intrigued by the thing you are offering, they will be more than charmed to realize what is acceptable with regards to the item, what is slightly below average, and how the item will help them.

At the point when you are suggesting a specific item, there are a few things to recall on the most proficient method to make it work viably and for your benefit. Sound like the valid and driving master in your field.

Recollect this straightforward condition: Price opposition decreases in direct extent to trust. On the off chance that your guests feel and accept that you are a specialist in your specialty, they are more disposed to making that buy. Then again, in case you are not radiating any certainty and confidence in supporting your items, they will presumably feel that same way and will go looking for another item or administration which is more acceptable.

How would you set up this emanation of skill? By offering novel and new arrangements they would not go anyplace else. Show evidence that what you are advancing functions as guaranteed. Show noticeable tributes and supports from regarded and known characters, in related fields obviously.

Stay away from publicity no matter what. It is smarter to sound serene and certain, than to shout and look for consideration. Also, you would not have any desire to sound amateurish and have that speculation adhere to your possible clients and customers, presently would you? Best to seem cool and confident simultaneously.

What's more, recollect; possibilities are not idiotic. They are really going to specialists and may definitely know the things that you know. In the event that you back up your cases with hard realities and information, they would happily put down hundreds, or even thousands worth of cash to your advancements. Be that as it may, in the event that you don't, they are adequately shrewd to attempt to check out your rivals and what they are advertising.

While suggesting an item, it is likewise significant that you give out special gifts. Individuals are now acquainted with the idea of offering gifts to advancing your own items.

Yet, not many individuals do this to advance affiliate items. Attempt to offer gifts that can advance or even have some data about your items or administrations.

Before you add proposals to you item, it is given that you should attempt to test the item and backing. Try not to risk advancing garbage items and administrations. Simply think what amount of time it required for you to construct validity and trust among your guests. All that will require to obliterate it is one serious mix-up on your part.

On the off chance that conceivable, have proposals of items that you have 100% trust in. Test the item support before you start to guarantee that individuals you are alluding it to would not be left between a rock and a hard place when an issue out of nowhere stimulate.

View your affiliate market and take a gander at the procedures you are utilizing. You may not be zeroing in on the proposals that your items need to have. You game plan is once in a while not by any means the only thing that is making your program works.

Attempt item suggestion and be among those rare sorts of people who have demonstrated its value.

Utilizing Camtasia to Increase Your Affiliate Checks

Since there are now bunches of individuals getting into affiliate showcasing, it is no big surprise that the opposition is getting hardened. The test is to attempt to outshine different affiliates and consider ways of having the option to achieve this.

There are additionally many tips and methods being instructed to these affiliate to best arrangement their system for their program to work adequately so more profit will be accomplished.

What better way of wowing your possibilities and clients than to record and distribute first rate, full movement and real time screen-caught recordings. In no way like inclination your persistent effort getting compensated by having your clients hopping up energetically in incredible expectation to purchase your item in that general area and afterward.

This is Camtasia in real life. It is a demonstrated truth; giving your clients something they can really see can detonate your internet based deals right away.

You don't have to have trainings and schooling to have the option to realize how this framework can function for your affiliate program. Anybody can make dazzling recordings, from sight and sound instructional exercises and bit by bit introductions accessible on the web. The interaction resembles having your clients situated close to you and checking out your work area, as you show them the things they need to see and hear. This done bit by bit.

For the people who doesn't have any acquaintance with it yet, how does Camtasia works?

It can record your work area movement in a solitary snap. No compelling reason to need to save and accumulate every one of your documents since it is recorded in that general area and afterward.

Can undoubtedly change over your recordings into site pages. When changed over you can have your clients visiting that specific page. Recordings are more obvious and take in dissimilar to perusing texts which in many cases is a taking a stab at thing to do.

Transfer your pages. Distribute them through online journals, RSS channel and webcasts. You might need your Camtasia's recordings to get around and contact others that might be possible clients later on. In no way like being apparent in many destinations and pages to promote yourself and get your message through.

There are different things you can do with your affiliate program utilizing Camtasia. You can...

Make dazzling sight and sound introductions that are demonstrated to expand deals since every one of the faculties are locked in. This additionally tends to lessen suspicion among fussy clients.

Diminish discounts and other client issues by exhibiting outwardly how to utilize your item and how to do it appropriately. Grievances will likewise be limited since the real factors and the show are there for the clients to simply see and find out about.

Advance affiliate items and administrations utilizing visual introductions. This is a compelling method of diverting your watchers directly to your affiliate site after they are done with the video. Benefit as much as possible from the show by placing your site area eventually and make them go there straightforwardly assuming they need more data.

Different your web-based closeout offers dramatically when you provide your perusers with a vibe of what you have to bring to the table.

Based from reports, barters that incorporates pictures builds offering rate by 400%. Envision how much higher it will be in case it were recordings.

Distribute significant infoproducts that you can sell at a lot greater expense. It will be all worth the value in light of the full hued designs menu and layouts that you will utilize.

Limit miscommunication with your clients. Quickly showing them what you need they needed in any case is causing them to see obviously the embodiment of your affiliate program. The beneficial thing about mixed media is, not a lot can turn out badly. It is there as of now.

These are only a portion of the things you can do with Camtasia that can be extremely useful in your picked affiliate program.

Note that the fundamental motivation behind utilizing Camtasia is to help the pay that is created from your affiliate program. Despite the fact that it tends to be utilized for amusement and pleasure purposes, which isn't actually a legitimate motivation behind why you decide to get all through that difficulty.

Attempt to zero in on the objective that you have set upon yourself to and accomplish that with the utilization of the things that might be a considerable amount of help in expanding your income.

Top 3 Ways To Boost Your Affiliate Commissions Overnight

The ideal universe of affiliate exhibiting doesn't require having your own site, overseeing customers, limits, thing improvement and backing. This is presumably the most un-requesting strategy for dispatching into a web based business and obtaining more advantages.

Expecting you are presently into an affiliate program, what may be the accompanying thing you could have to do? Twofold, or even triple, your rewards, right? How might you do that?

Here are some stunning tips on the most ideal way of supporting your affiliate program installments present moment.

1. Know the best program and things to progress.

Plainly, you would have to propel a program that will engage you to achieve the best advantages in the briefest possible time.

There are a couple of components to consider in picking such a program. Pick the ones that have a liberal commission structure. Have things that fit in with your ideal vested party. Likewise, that has a solid history of paying their affiliate successfully and on time. If you can't seem to extend your hypotheses, dump that program and keep on looking for better ones.

There are huge number of affiliate programs online which gives you the inspiration to be particular. You may have to pick the best to keep away from losing your publicizing dollars.

Form free reports or short E-Books to pass on from your site. There is an unbelievable possibility that you are equaling various affiliates that are propelling a comparable program. If you start forming short report related to the thing you are propelling, you will really need to isolate yourself from various affiliates.

In the reports, give some significant information to free. In case possible, add a couple of ideas about the things. With E-Books, you get legitimacy. Customers will see that in you and they will be enamored to assess what you are publicizing.

2. Collect and save the email areas of the people who download your free E-Books.

It's unquestionably a fact that people don't make a purchase on the chief mentioning. You may have to pass on your message in overabundance of numerous occasions to make an arrangement.

This is the fundamental inspiration driving why you should accumulate the contact information of individuals who downloaded your reports and E-Books. You can make ensuing meet-ups on these contacts to remind them to make a purchase from you.

Get the contact information of a chance preceding sending them to the vender's site. Recollect that you are without giving advancement to the thing owners. You get repaid exactly when you make an arrangement. If you send prospects clearly to the dealers, chances are they would be lost to you forever.

However, when you get their names, you can for the most part send other publicizing messages to them to have the choice to get a ceaseless commission as opposed to a one-time bargain so to speak.

Appropriate a web based notice or E-zine. It is for each situation best to recommend a thing to someone you know than to present to an untouchable. This is the purpose for disseminating your own flyer. This furthermore allows you to cultivate a relationship subject to endow with your endorsers.

This framework is a delicate agreement between outfitting important information with an endeavor to sell something. In case you continue to make informational distributions you will really need to collect a sensation of correspondence in your perusers that may lead them to help you by buying your things.

3. Solicitation higher than customary commission from brokers.

In the event that you are currently productive with a particular progression, you should endeavor to advance toward the seller and organize a rate commission for your arrangements.

If the seller is sharp, the person being referred to will likely yield your requesting rather than lose a significant asset in you. Recollect that you are a zero-danger hypothesis to your transporter; so don't be timid about referencing for extension in your rewards. Essentially endeavor to be reasonable concerning it.

Create strong remuneration Per Click notices. PPC web record is the best strategy for advancing on the web. As an affiliate, you can make a little compensation just by supervising PPC missions like Google AdWords and Overture. Then, you should endeavor to screen them to see which advancements are more effective and which ones to dispose of.

Assess these techniques and see the qualification it can make to your extra checks in the briefest of time.

Instructions to Avoid The 3 Most Common Affiliate Mistakes

As the handbook attracts to a close to end and shutting distribution, here are some peril signs and hazardous waters you shouldn't step on in the affiliate promoting scene!

So tune in up...

Affiliate promoting is one of the best and amazing methods of bringing in some cash on the web. This program allows everyone an opportunity to create a gain through the Internet. Since these affiliate advertising programs are not difficult to join, carry out and pays a commission consistently, more an additional group are currently willing around here.

Notwithstanding, similar to all organizations, there are bunches of traps in the affiliate promoting business. Submitting the absolute most normal missteps will cost the advertisers a huge part taken from the benefit they are making each day. That is the reason it is smarter to keep away from them than be remorseful eventually.

Mix-up number 1: Choosing some unacceptable affiliate.

Many individuals need to procure from affiliate showcasing as quick as could be expected. In their race to be important for one, they will in general pick a trend item. This is the sort of items that the program believes is "hot". They pick the item that is popular without really considering if the item requests to them. This is certifiably not an exceptionally savvy move clearly.

Rather than getting on board with that fad, attempt to pick an item in which you are really keen on. For any undertaking to succeed, you should set aside some effort to plan and sort out your activities.

Pick an item that requests to you. Then, at that point, do some examination concerning that item to check whether they are sought after. Advancing an item you are more energetic about is simpler than advancing one for the income as it were.

Mix-up number 2: Joining too many affiliate programs.

Since affiliate programs are extremely simple to go along with, you may be enticed to join products of affiliate projects to attempt to augment the income you will get. Other than you might feel that everything is all good and nothing to lose by being essential for some affiliate programs.

Valid, that is an extraordinary way of having numerous types of revenue. Nonetheless, joining different projects and endeavoring to advance them all simultaneously will keep you from focusing on every single one of them.

The outcome? The most extreme capability of your affiliate program isn't understood and the pay created won't by and large be just about as tremendous as you were suspecting at first it would. The most ideal way of getting incredible outcome is by joining only one program that pays a 40% commission at any rate. Then, at that point, give it your best exertion by advancing your items excitedly. When you see that it is creating a sensible gain, then, at that point, perhaps you would now be able to join another affiliate program.

The method is to do it gradually. There is actually no compelling reason to hurry into things, particularly with affiliate showcasing. With the status quo going, what's to come is looking truly brilliant and it appears affiliate promoting will remain for quite a while as well.

Slip-up number 3: Not accepting the item or utilizing the help.

As an affiliate, you primary design is to successfully and convincingly advance an item or administration and to discover clients. For you to accomplish this reason, you should have the option to hand-off to the clients that specific item and administration. It is thusly hard for you to do this when you, when all is said and done, have not given these things a shot. In this way, you will neglect to advance and suggest them convincingly. You will likewise neglect to make a longing in your clients to profit any of what you are advertising.

Attempt the item or administration by and by first before you join as an affiliate to check whether it is truly conveying what it guarantees. On the off chance that you have done as such, you are one of the dependable and living confirmations mindful of its benefits and inconveniences. Your clients will then, at that point, feel the genuineness and honesty in you and this will trigger them to give them a shot for themselves.

Many affiliate advertisers commit these errors and are paying the consequences for their activities. To not fall into a similar circumstance they have been in, attempt to do everything to try not to mess up the same way.

Time is the key. Set aside the effort to dissect your promoting system and check in case you are in the right track. Whenever done appropriately, you will actually want to amplify your affiliate advertising program and acquire higher benefits.

Don't miss out!

Visit the website below and you can sign up to receive emails whenever Jim Stephens publishes a new book. There's no charge and no obligation.

https://books2read.com/r/B-A-VNEK-YGATB

BOOKS 2 READ

Connecting independent readers to independent writers.

Also by Jim Stephens

Kindle Publishing Made Easy: Autopilot Cash With Amazon Kindle!
Million-Dollar Secrets of the Amazon Associates: How They Make Money From the Biggest Online Shopping Mall
Self-Publishing Made Easy: The Easy Way to Self-publish Your Own Books!
Scam Busters: How to Avoid the Most Popular Scams of Today!
Affiliate Marketing and Blogging
The Quick and Easy Guide of Diamonds
Government Information
Hiking and Camping
Koi Pond
Law Information Guide
Motor Homes Research
Affiliate Marketing and Success Systems
Online Shopping
Outsourcing Ebooks and Software Jobs
Personal Loans
Private Jet Charters
Private Yacht Charters
Affiliate Marketing Blueprint

About the Publisher

Accepting manuscripts in the most categories. We love to help people get their words available to the world.

Revival Waves of Glory focus is to provide more options to be published. We do traditional paperbacks, hardcovers, audio books and ebooks all over the world. A traditional royalty-based publisher that offers self-publishing options, Revival Waves provides a very author friendly and transparent publishing process, with President Bill Vincent involved in the full process of your book. Send us your manuscript and we will contact you as soon as possible.

Contact: Bill Vincent at rwgpublishing@yahoo.com www.rwgpublishing.com

www.ingramcontent.com/pod-product-compliance
Lightning Source LLC
LaVergne TN
LVHW042003060526
838200LV00041B/1851